Bird on a Fence Post

A Prose Poetry Collection

by

Rose Anne Dane

Cover art by Mark A. Messing

For information regarding permission, write:
Dancing Rose Books (Rose Dane)
4864 Lancaster Dr. NE #250
Salem, OR 97305

ISBN-13: 978-0-9796147-0-5
ISBN-10: 0-9796147-0-8

Dane, Rose Anne
    Bird on a fence post : a prose poetry collection / by
Rose Anne Dane ; cover art by Mark A. Messing.
    p. cm.
    ISBN-13: 978-0-9796147-0-5
    ISBN-10: 0-9796147-0-8

    I. Messing, Mark A. II. Title.

PS3604.A522B57 2007   811'.6
                   QBI07-7007135

Bird on a Fence Post

Dancing Rose Books
www.dancingrosebooks.com

Your Town Press, Printers
2773 Cherry Avenue NE
Salem, OR 97303

CONTENTS

CONTENTS

ACKNOWLEDGEMENTS

Many thanks to my husband, Peter J. Dane, who has been so patient during my poetry book project. It has involved a great deal of time, along with manuscript pages scattered about all over the floor.

Thanks to my many friends who have encouraged me to keep it up, and get the book done.

My gratitude for a job well done is also extended to Trudy McKinnell of PageWorks Graphic Design who laid out the book and placed the charming graphics in all the right places.

Dennis Scott, manager of Your Town Press, is also appreciated for his suggestions and advice, as well as printing the poetry book in a professional manner.

ABOUT THE AUTHOR

"Flexible is my middle name," says Rose Anne Dane.
Her life has demanded flexibility through the years. She
has lived in South Dakota, Oregon, Washington, California,
Utah, Colorado, Nevada and on the island of Guam, USA.

All of this moving around has involved packing boxes,
loading up cars, negotiating moving trucks and studying
the latest maps. She has often relished making friends
in new communities.

Ms. Dane has a diversified employment history; work as a
car hop, waitress, receptionist, secretary, and nanny. She
has also worked as a cashier, substitute school teacher,
feature writer, sales professional and health spa instructor.

She is a graduate of Portland Community College in
Oregon with an associate degree in Business Management.

An avid supporter of Toastmasters International, Rose has
been a leader in assorted clubs. She has been a prize-
winning speaker and seminar facilitator.

The author is married to Peter J. Dane and they've had
many shared adventures. She cherishes her three children
from a previous marriage and her four grandsons.

ABOUT THE Book COVER ARTIST

Mark A. Messing created the charming meadowlark cover, inspired by the poem, "Bird on a Fence Post." This poem was chosen as a favorite of Reno, Nevada residents during a 'Cowboy Poetry' contest.

Messing's custom paintings, vivid murals and unique designs adorn some of Nevada's finest homes and businesses. One of his most outstanding murals is on display at Bally's Casino in Las Vegas. It is located at the main swimming pool and it features a tropical island with marvelous details.

Mark recently moved back to Salem, Oregon. He is discovering the beauty of Oregon in a new, refreshing way.

INTRODUCTION

What could be more exciting than creating a prose poetry book? My poems were written during several years of personal challenge, numerous changes in my life and getting in touch with my inner self.

As a curious ten year old, one of my favorite activities was to look in the Webster's Dictionary, copying down unique vocabulary words. It was then that I took an interest in expressing my ideas through the written word.

As a young mother in Beaverton, Oregon, I worked as a feature writer for 'The Valley Times' newspaper. I would explore the town, in search of interesting people. Then I would interview them, type up my notes and submit the article to the women's editor by Wednesday of each week.

My fascination with prose poetry began when I took a few creative writing classes at Portland Community College. During the ensuing years, if I traveled to an exotic place, I'd challenge myself to get out my ball point pen and compose a description that took in the sights, sounds and the atmosphere.

An added touch to the book is the Vocabulary Word List, inviting readers to find each one in the book. Enjoy the word pictures that I have painted for you.

May your love of poetry increase as you take this literary journey.

-Rose Anne Dane-

Can you find these vocabulary words?

aloof	ambling	apprehension
aura	basking	beguiling
bulwark	capacious	cataclysm
cosmopolitan	crustacean	delectable
elusive	encompasses	enmeshed
entrenched	exquisite	furtively
garbled	gingerly	gnarled
jauntily	jostled	laboriously
looming	lumbering	meander
muster	nocturnal	ocotillo
ominous	peering	pensively
permeates	precariously	profusely
raucous	rejuvenation	roached
saunters	settee	sultry
sustenance	talons	tantalizing
traipsing	wafting	wistfully

Travels, Tales and Adventures

Lychee Nuts

Wandering up and down the streets and alleys of teeming,
bustling Hong Kong Island.

So many people: smiling, friendly, sad, and sometimes
quite aloof. So many different colors of faces in the
vigorously moving crowds.

Riding a huge dull-green ferry boat, while gently bobbing
on murky gray water to "the other side" – Kowloon
Island, that is.

Enjoying shopping in a cluster of stores, viewing a
multitude of precious treasures. There are elegantly
beaded sweaters, appealing jade figurines and some
delicately painted porcelain.

An American business man that we recognize comes
into view. "How about a snack?" he says, as he takes
us by the arms, suspecting that we have never tasted
any lychee nuts.

He buys a small bunch of the red fruit as I say: "Looks
like a dark strawberry!" "Try it," he says, with a grin.
I wrinkle up my nose, as if in doubt.

"Does it taste good?"

I cautiously bite into the fruit. It is hard; almost hurts
my teeth. Then all of us go on down the street while we
eat the firm, exotic lychee nuts.

Trolley Car Memories

Memories of a trolley car ride – smelling the crisp,
early morning air.

Patiently waiting near funny, winding tracks in the
big-city streets, while munching on a hurriedly
prepared piece of toast.

Here it comes, the trolley is moving along the rugged
tracks, quick as can be. Strange-looking electric wires
above us all efficiently control the lumbering trolley cars.

"Climb up the steps, folks – everyone in?" the alert
conductor cheerfully asks many eager riders.

Sitting in a comfortable seat while contemplating the
day ahead. A twenty-minute run and the trolley ride
is done.

Off, down the steps and into the street – to work and
to marvel in the large city, the exciting, vibrant city of
Los Angeles, California.

Seaside, Oregon

A wide, multi-colored rainbow with hues of pink, yellow, blue, lavender and a nice blending of other colors – cheering up the slate gray sky line as light rain drops are mingled with rays of sparkling sunlight.

Avenue A, Columbia Street, South Downing and more can be viewed by curious tourists. A sign near BPOE Seaside 1748 announces: Stuffed Pork Chops Dinner.

A car parked along South Edgewood has a North Dakota license plate on it. Another car is parked in front of a dinky residential apartment building, with a license plate that says, Guam, USA.

Unique shops and cafes or restaurants, all snuggled together on Broadway street, located in the hub of pedestrian traffic. All sorts of visitors are urged to come inside, to view the fine wares.

Windansea, Sea Trader Imports and Alpine Garden Restaurant, plus Seaside Agate and Gift Shop; all of them are such fascinating places. There is David's Fine Porcelain and Bridge Tender Tavern, too.

Seaside City Hall; an old, rustic red building that is very plain and square-shaped. It is a charming tie-in of the city's past with it's present.

Seaside Flea Market, near Roosevelt and Broadway has many fine collectibles and dishes. A huge multi-faceted collection of antiques sits inside of the capacious building, one of the best places ever.

Oceanway Street: so appealing. The city has clean streets with no trash lying around. Residents can be justifiably proud of their pleasant ocean-side community.

Cozy motels, bed and breakfast inns, little house rentals; fine places to stay for one night, a week, a month. Shilo Inn is elegant. Best Western Seashore Resort Motel and others offer peaceful sleep and enchanting ocean views.

The beachcomber, taking delight in smooth sand as it tends to instantly slip through bare toes, frolics playfully near gently lapping waves. She smells fresh, tingling air as it penetrates her lungs, then she looks away, toward polished houses, lined up along small cliffs perched above the scenic Oregon beach.

She notices how the houses vary from one another in style and colors: white, pewter, blue, gray, beige, pale peach, rusty red and one that stands out from the rest, displaying a bold green mist window trim.

A seagull finds tender morsels from a stranded crab, his bottom half stuck in the dark wet sand as the incoming tidal waves sweep over him, then release him, exposed to constant pecking of the pale gray hungry bird.

In a moment there are eight clamoring seagulls, gathered around the helpless crab. Raucous calls can be heard as a fight ensues.

Suddenly a daring bird darts forward, drags the crab away, soars into the air, then drops his prey and stabs at it with his powerful beak as the water lurches forward, then covers the dead crustacean.

Children are riding a strange contraption. Teenagers are riding them too. Parents and grandparents join right in. They tend to giggle with excitement as they ride up and down the shore: three-wheeled pedal bikes, they're called.

Other people prefer mopeds, those sleek motorized scooters. It looks like great fun as they blend in with the traffic flow, then change lanes, and speed forward with ease.

Fabulous Seaside, Oregon: worthy of it's name. What could be more inviting – or so much fun? It's truly a city of interest to people from around the world.

Filipino Cowboy

High in the cloudless sky upon the scenic mountain in cool, tantalizing air rides a young man on his beautiful red horse.

Cowboy hat, blue denim jacket, hardy and rough jeans with high-heeled boots in strong stirrups. A brown-faced cowboy can be seen.

Baguio, charming and serene elevated mountain town that looks like a picture from Switzerland, enmeshed in fragrant pine trees. This is the young man's home, the only home he has ever known.

A little boy of four who has dark-blond hair and wondering blue eyes, wants a ride on the sleek, red horse.

"How much – how many pesos?" asks his father, an American tourist. A bargain is made, the men agree.

Up and down smooth round hills, covered with short, cutting grass. The two of them disappear on the horizon. Suddenly, they appear again, very briefly.

The watching parents can see the Filipino cowboy, holding on to the black reins, his protecting arms draped around their precious son.

The horse returns to the spot from which he started.
A delighted, happy look is on the small boy's face.

"That ride was fun!" he says, with a broad smile.
Then: goodbyes are said by all.

Plumeria and Banyan Trees

Tiny, delicate gray doves busy pecking away at reddish-brown dirt on the ground –

Fresh, sun-ripened pineapples, taken out of vast bush-covered fields, full of delicious yellow sugar spots –

Tall, thick green sugar cane, presenting a sharp, cutting bulwark against any would-be intruders –

Bright pale gold flecks of gritty sand on inviting, warm beaches along with hard, small rocks that people step on as they prepare for a swim in gently lapping water –

Soft, fragrant smelling tropical breezes, caressing new tourists and residents alike, a welcome relief from sultry hotel rooms –

White plumeria flowers, thriving on tree limbs throughout Oahu, hard and firm, plucked off by people and used for decorative leis –

In the early evening sunset, swimmers are still playing in the salty, rolling surf, keeping out of the way of a narrow and silent outrigger canoe, manned by six strong men -

Bus rides for only thirty five cents: anywhere on the whole island. So many places to go to, so many things to see and do – such as visit the Zoo.

Renting a car, looking at such streets as Nuuanu Avenue, Alakea Street and Ala Wai Boulevard, funny-sounding names to us –

A ride in a Glass Bottom Boat, glancing at wiggly fish, noticing with delight playful dolphins nearby, jumping around us in gently swirling ocean waves –

An elegant dinner cruise in a romantic star-studded sky, quietly gliding along in shimmering water, aboard a luminous, highly polished yacht –

Paradise Park, full of vividly colored birds that whistle and dart from one tree to another –

Waimea Falls Park, entrenched by deep green tropical plants and unique trees, such as a huge Banyan. It has strange looking rope-like branches that hang down everywhere.

An awesome waterfall is a sight to behold: 45 feet of cascading water. Wow! Some daring people actually play in the frothy water below.

Ala Moana Shopping Center, full of typical stores that so many people know: Penney's, Sears, Liberty House. There are handy places to grab a hasty meal: McDonald's, KFC and others. Assorted shops show off exotic treasures from the Philippines, Japan and Hong Kong –

Coconut syrup on pancakes in the morning – tasting
simply terrific.

Lunch time finally arrives.
"Who wants some coconut ice cream?" "We do!"

Fun-loving visitors swarming around Waikiki Beach,
most of them dressed in skimpy swim wear, jauntily
carrying beach bags or nicely glazed surfboards –

Women love their long, gracefully flowing dresses – or
short ones, splashed with blues, greens, even purple –
muumuus, they're called.

Men feel cool in their flower-patterned polish cotton
shirts, sporting blues, greens, yellows and colors of
the rainbow.

Friendly, smiling Hawaiians acknowledge us as they walk
by. They seem to say, "Welcome to my tropical paradise –
my home."

Alpha and Omega

On that fateful day in the year 2122 – I planted my feet on the world anew. For two years we had traveled through time and thick, deep space. We were the last survivors of the human race.

The apocalypse that had destroyed our earth was an omen that would bring on new birth – for as the roaring cataclysm started and was foreseen, many of the world's scholars in their rush to be seen, developed a ship that we named "The Dorreen."

Those of us who were the chosen few, had the minds and strength to make a crew. And we knew as she sat on her pad, that she had the strength and power that we could command.

For she was The Dorreen, a majestic lady; she could go forth and come back from "the fire of Hades." But alas, that is what earth, green, sweet Mother Earth would go through: and we knew, yes, we knew.

Early on the morning of the twenty-third, a message came on the wings of a great white bird. It was time to leave – to head for the stars. The earth's fate was woven, and so was ours.

Dorreen sat silently as we went through her doors. Her systems were fine and so were her stores. We checked her power and made sure that everyone was in place. Then we began the countdown that would save our race.

Her engines roared and her rockets flared. She left the launching pad and soared into the air. We left the earth and slowly looked behind us. We were afraid that the destruction would surely find us.

I felt strange, sitting there – watching the earth go up in awful flames. First it turned orange, then chalky white. Very soon it disappeared. But we had to go on – and go on, we did, for now it was time to populate the new planet; like the earth we once did.

Note: this poem was written by Mark A. Messing, son of Rose Dane.

Desert Delights
Palm Springs, California

A cute little cottontail rabbit was munching on lush green grass, right next to Coco's Restaurant. I could hardly believe my eyes. Traffic was moving rather quickly at Smoke Tree Lane and East Palm Canyon, but there she sat, furtively glancing at me.

I did my best to stand very still for a few moments, then I slowly inched closer to her. Reluctantly, she scampered into some bushes. What a treat: seeing not one, but two cottontails that day.

A happy hummingbird visits me often, right in front of my patio door. He flits about, from one flower-laden bush to another, gathering sustenance during that day.

His black-topped head is visible, yet his tiny wings appear to be invisible as I try to watch him, speeding about like a flash of light. What a pleasure it is to catch his happy mood!

In the early morning, when I get up and glance out of my windows, many elegant palm trees are in view, scattered along the street. I can hardly wait to go outside for my daily walk.

As I meander down the streets, I see huge cacti, orange trees, lemon trees, a huge patch of rich magenta bougainvillea, and mail boxes.

Then there are yellow snapdragons, lavender pansies, thorny ocotillo and clusters of flowers in every direction.

It is good to embrace my desert world, full of desert delights.

San Francisco Sights

A young miss, only seventeen, slowly walks along
dull-gray sidewalks, while occasionally pausing to
smell swirling fresh air, gaily blowing in from the
Pacific Ocean.

A sense of pleasure permeates her body as she soaks
up the warmth of a lazy afternoon sun. She decides to
walk on, traipsing up and down gently sloping hills, while
exercising her strong legs.

Freshly painted apartment buildings and Victorian-style
houses fascinate her. She likes to see bright pink, red
and yellow flowers that decorate many large porches.

At the uppermost hill, not far from Green Street – she
looks down and all around the city. It is just an amazing
sight: tall skyscrapers, parks, small stores, blue water and
assorted houses.

Never-ending streets seem to weave their way up and
down – like a set of narrow ribbons. She relishes the
cosmopolitan mood of the city, the community-minded
spirit displayed by people who tend to live side by side,
representing numerous nations of the world.

The sun's rays are penetrating her back, her arms, even
her shoulders. It is getting hot as time slips by. She
hears a dog barking in the distance and a gentle babbling
of voices as she saunters past an inviting park.

Mournful-sounding fog horns whistle loudly amidst tossing, churning ocean waters. The horns are not constant, but can be heard every few minutes; spreading their warning about dangerously deep water.

It feels like a magnet is pulling her to explore some more. She is compelled to change directions, to stroll toward the bay. She wants to gaze at sleek sailboats and rugged fishing boats, adorned with rolls of thick rope at Fisherman's Wharf.

At last – she's there, scanning over the sights, taking in the sounds. A collection of boats with such names as "Charlene" – "Athena" – and "Moonstruck" are securely tied to slowly rocking docks, proudly arranged in an orderly manner.

Oh, to bounce along the rippling waves some day!

The seventeen-year old thinks how good it is to claim this enchanting bay, the large, sparkling city as her very own, the city of San Francisco, California.

Open Observations

A Familiar Face

A familiar face is good to see, a familiar face to you
and me.

Living in a world of quiet solitude, that has its merits –
But! A familiar face is nice to see.

Surrounded by rushing crowds, people ambling by.
A person could be a stranger in a cold world; and
then – a familiar face. Oh, how very good to see!

Be Glad, My Friend

Be glad for who you are, my friend, my special friend.
When you are "down" – manage to smile anyway.
Muster up the strength to say, "I am glad that I am me."

Be glad when you are "up" and the soothing sun seems
to shine all day. Do be glad. Have a thankful heart.
Dance to the gentle breezes and say, "I am – me."

Who is like you? – no one, my friend. Not one single
person in this whole wide world is exactly like you.
Wow! What could be more amazing than that?

Your chin, your smile, the shape of your eyelids, and
the unique personality you possess: in God's plan, you
are valued as one very special human miracle. Yes!

Be glad, my friend, my special friend. Go ahead: take
the time to gaze into a mirror today. Really see yourself.
Declare to your reflection: "I am glad – that I am me."

Different, Somehow
Oaks Park Roller Rink - Portland, Oregon

Whirling whirling round and round, the happy skaters
whiz along. Click click sound of roller skates can be
heard in the noisy rink.

People in the observation area scan the scene, turning
their heads from side to side.

They see girls in short satin skirts and pretty blouses –
boys in blue jeans and neat shirts. Black skates and white
skates are on the feet of quickly circling skaters.

Organ music is played in happy, lilting rhythm. The
organist in his glass-covered spot seems to smile a lot
as he watches the charged-up group going round and
round.

Flashing neon lights blink on and off near the ceiling:
Couples only; All skate; Trio only. Everyone obeys
the signs as they glide along shiny smooth wood floors
in the cheerful rink.

All appears normal to the viewers, until they notice three
teenagers holding hands, valiantly trying to avoid falling
down. It appears that they are precariously staying up,
yet strong, confidant, at ease.

They are different, somehow. Yes, that's it:
they are blind.

Recipe for Success and Happiness

The successful person is one who sets goals and then accomplishes them;

Who starts a project and completes it;

Who puts as much of himself into work, school, or sports as he possibly can.

The happy person is one who gives more than he expects to receive;

Who uses words of kindness freely;

Who dares to express his own ideas and not apologize for them;

Who has a sense of humor when facing life's difficult problems;

Who does not wish for no problems, but finds logical answers to the ones he does have.

Romantic Reflections

The Eraser

We had spent a wonderful year together, best of friends
and lovers too, you and I. You made me laugh, you made
me cry.

You gave me your heart, your kisses too. I loved to see
your warm smile, just for me alone.

Oh, I could be 'down' – but you would often cheer me up,
encouraging me and getting me to laugh out loud. My
days were filled with warm sunshine.

You were so good to me, so kind. "Dusty Rose" was what
you called me, as you scooped me up in your waiting arms.

When we walked together, it was a bit awkward. It looked
like we didn't 'fit' – or so it seemed. You were so tall and
I was so short.

Yet people would look at us and smile tenderly. They
seemed to sense our harmonious ways - enjoying each
other's company, holding hands: looking into each other's
eyes, you and I.

Pretty cards were exchanged, nice gifts too. Holidays were
fun and trips were taken: adventures shared by two. Work
times and play times; we were so special, you and I.

One cold dreary day, it was different, somehow. I moved
to a place of my own, hoping that you would plead with me,
to say: "We can work this out. Let's be together, please."

But you did not call. You didn't drop by. I felt so all alone.
Could it be that you were trying to erase me from your life?

We would see one another occasionally. Our paths would
cross and we'd say to each other, "Hi, how are you doing?"
It was always so brief, so fleeting. That was all.

I shed many free-flowing tears. I gulped real hard when
I drove near your little house, but I figured that I would use
an eraser too.

I would get out that blackboard and scrub it and scrub it
with a dirty old eraser. I would find someone else – yes,
I would.

In a few short weeks I made some new friends. I had
some dates with good-looking guys. Then I found 'him',
a special man – the new love of my life.

We shared warm kisses, dancing ballroom style. There
were enchanting moonlight walks. The eraser was starting
to work.

So more time went by – good friend, Father Time. You
were just a fading memory. Impulsively, one day I picked
up a telephone to give you a hesitant call.

The sound of your voice was like music to my ears.
"I miss you, I miss the way you made me laugh,"
I suddenly blurted out.

"I miss you too," was your soft reply. We talked some
more and after I hung up the telephone, I saw that
eraser feebly trying to move, struggling to finally erase
you from my life.

Underneath the dark smudges I saw something on the
blackboard. I was looking inward, at my very deepest
heart. The words said:
    I miss you – so much, so very much.

Love in Winter

Her name is Mary. His name is Harold. They walk
toward each other, slowly and laboriously across the
shiny, clean floor.

Her eyes twinkle with delight, for she has a marvelous
idea. His eyes twinkle too, for he has something
wonderful on his mind.

Mary steadies herself by moving her cane a bit closer to
her hips. Harold shuffles his feet a bit livelier as they
meet face to face, within inches of each other.

He bends forward, toward her gently lined face, while
she bends toward his big blue eyes. Then their lips meet
softly. He hesitates, steps back, revealing a happy feeling,
which is evident to the small group of residents gathered
nearby.

She gingerly moves a few steps away from him. Her
face takes on a special glow, as if she is listening to a
tenderly romantic song. Again, their warm lips meet,
but this time the kiss is stronger.

The nursing home receptionist watches them from her
small desk and smiles to herself.

She realizes that romance is there – why, it's everywhere!

Their hair is silver-white and growing wrinkles cannot be disguised.

The mind is sometimes hazy with remembrances of frisky youth so long ago.

But love is alive; alive and well, in the Winter Time of life.

A Bag of Popcorn

Popcorn jumped out from the machine, flowing over the
rim of the heavy pot. Yellow-white kernels could be seen
in large plastic sacks stacked nearby, ready for use.
The concessions cashier kept busy, serving customers in
the theater lobby.

She was 18-years old and thrilled with big city life. Her
days were filled with bus rides to ballet classes, places
to explore, chores to do at the boarding house and
busy people.

Wearing a crisp white cap, a young sailor approached the
snack counter. "Hi!" I'll have a bag of popcorn," he
said cheerfully.

Her hands deftly moved, grabbing for the bag, while she
quickly glanced at him. The perky girl admired his brown
wavy hair and his blue eyes with long eyelashes – in a
gentle, appealing face.

"My name is Phil – what's yours?"
Without any hesitation, she replied "Annie."
He smiled broadly. "Where you from?"
"I'm from Salem, Oregon," she answered.

"Really? I'm from Seattle, Washington. See you," he
said, as he darted behind a curtain to see the movie.
Her heart seemed to skip a few beats as she thought
about their light conversation.

Intermission time finally arrived. The blob of bodies
shoved forward.

"Hersheys candy bar, please – and a small coke."
"Two bags of popcorn and some salted peanuts."
The raucous voices around her became a constantly
buzzing sound.

At last, the theater patrons returned to their seats.
Annie was surprised to see the sailor standing at her
counter again. "Hi," he said, dazzling her with his
warm smile.

"Where do you live?" She blushed slightly.
"On Green Street, I get there by bus."
"I'd like to walk you home," he sweetly offered.
"That would be nice, I'll think about it."

When the flick ended, the crowd jostled each other as
they went out of the big doors, rubbing their eyes to
get used to the San Francisco lights and rushing traffic.

Phil patiently waited for her to clean off the counters
and make sure that she put everything away where it
belonged.

They clambered aboard a long city bus, headed for the
bay. City lights were very bright as they sat side by side,
strangers – yet not. She liked his company and she felt
comfortable with him.

After getting off the bus, the two of them walked down serene hills to the waiting sand. Sea water could be heard, harshly lapping against jagged rocks as it rushed forward to the shore.

The young couple peered up into the darkened sky, dotted with brightly twinkling stars and romantic, silvery-streaked moonlight; moonlight to walk by, moonlight to help them look at each other.

Let's sit on this big smooth rock," he suggested. As they talked, he slipped his hands around hers. They kissed gently on the lips. Then Phil suddenly stood up.

"Do you realize what time it is?"
"No, but I guess it's about two o'clock in the morning."

The caring Navy man expressed concern. "You're right, I've got to get you home."

When they arrived at the immense white boarding house, he drew her close to his chest, kissing her well.

He released her on the porch as a somber look shadowed his face. "Annie, you're too trusting." Startled by his mood change, she asked, "What do you mean by that?"

"I mean – here I am, a stranger and you let me be alone with you, at the deserted beach. Don't you know that I could have beat you up – or something worse, and no one would have known what happened?"

She felt embarrassed as he stroked her hair, then he gently touched her upturned face.

"I didn't mean to scare you, I just said that for your own good."

"Goodnight," she said, softly.
"Goodnight," he replied, and in a moment he was off the porch, hastily walking down the sidewalk.

She scooted inside of the house and tiptoed to her nicely furnished bedroom. Not a single person stirred.

They saw each other again, although briefly. In no time at all, her handsome sailor was aboard his ship: lonely, wondering about his future. And she went back to her folks in Oregon.

Letters flew back and forth, a sharing of thoughts in ink. Messages to each other tapered off, then there were none.

Phil sometimes wondered what happened to the Popcorn Girl; the girl he met in a movie theater – and Annie would wonder where he was, as he sailed on mighty ocean waves.

She smiled as she recalled how he walked with her on a starlit night, holding her hand as they strolled by the San Francisco Bay.

Nonpareil Nevada

An Artist's Palette
October 1, 1998

The time is 6:35 in the evening and a brisk, refreshing breeze is blowing from the north.

I look out of my picture window and delight in what I see. Clouds are everywhere, huge white 'snow-like clouds' forming in a long, luxurious row are slowly moving to the left of me.

There is a wonderful artist's palette of blue, purple, silver and white steaks, all blending together in fancy swirls that move from left to right and back to the left.

Tiny lavender blue clouds, a bunch of them, proudly display their beauty in the early evening air here in Reno, Nevada. Free-spirited seagulls, funny ducks and elegant gray geese soar effortlessly through the dusky sky.

Colors fade and change within a few short minutes: now I see streaks of soft, very pale pink above the deep blue mountain ridges to the west and an interesting pastel blue sky near the high hills.

Moist, haze-splashed clouds cluster above towering Mount Rose at the far south end of the city.

Oh, I enjoy Nevada skies so much – so very much.

Sweet Air of Spring

It is April and fresh, wonderfully sweet air is wafting along, while customers shop at Albertson's Market, near McCarran Boulevard.

I pause and ignore the chores that should be done to gaze in wonderment at the changing sky. Exquisite pink streaks caress pastel blue clouds in the eastern sky, near the city of Sparks.

I get in my car and drive to a pleasant pasture. As I place my elbows on a faded gray fence, I sense refreshing renewal this Spring evening as interesting birds pursue assorted activities.

Peach-breasted robins happily gather in small groups, as they rapidly rush from one spot to another, seeking some last bits of nourishment before darkness sets in.

Delicate charming quail with funny head ornaments tend to scamper from one location to another, reveling in softly blowing breezes.

Oh, blessed Spring. It's here at last!

-Rose Anne Dane-

Bird on a Fence Post

When I was ten years old and walking through grassy pastures, I heard a wonderful song.

A yellow bird was sitting on an old fence post, singing so happily.

When I got back to the farm house, I asked my mother:

"What is the name of that pretty yellow bird?"
"Oh, that's a Meadow Lark," she quickly replied.

Recently I went hiking in the Reno hills, covered with sagebrush and dusty trails. It was quiet, so very quiet.

Then I heard a familiar sound: a Meadow Lark was singing his song to me, as he flew from one fence post to another.

I listened for a long time, basking in the melody of his happy song, just like the one that I heard when I was only ten.

Note: This poem was chosen as a favorite by Reno, Nevada residents during a Cowboy Poetry contest.

The author read her poem at The Peppermill Casino showroom on June 26, 1999.

December Enchantment

Sparkling white snow could be seen on all the hills and the mountain that protectively surrounded the city. Set against the crisp, blue sky, it was a wondrous sight.

As I walked down Linda Way, near Greg Street in Sparks, Nevada, a huge black and white magpie vigorously squawked at me while clinging to upper branches in a very tall tree.

I enjoyed the crunchy sounds made by my own footsteps in snow-covered rocks and walkways. A magnificent pine tree stood in the cold morning air as I leisurely walked underneath it's strong branches.

What was the temperature right now? It seemed to be around 34 degrees or so, as I blew misty vapors out of my cool lips.

Although it was 10:15 in the morning, a beguiling round-shaped moon was still visible in the far-away sky; half of the circle was covered by a dense blue color; the other half, a mixture of white and pastel blue.

As I strolled a few blocks to my destination, the gentle warmth of my gloves felt good. My cheeks and ears were changing from cozy warm to tingly cold, but I did not mind: it was a truly perfect December day.

Penthouse Suite at The Mirage

Wow! This room number 30-060 is one of the swankiest ones that I've ever seen in my life. Located on the penthouse floor of The Mirage Hotel, it's nice, very nice.

Security guards protect exclusive elevators, labeled A to E. No one is allowed entrance to the area without permission. Las Vegas hotels can be awesome, all right.

I marvel at the lovely suite that I'm babysitting in – what a privilege! An elegantly framed picture of roses in a blue vase hangs on one wall.

Cheerful primary colors of red, yellow and blue with black accents abound throughout this magnificent two-bedroom suite that has a living area in the middle of the main room.

I like the entry way, which has a handy settee below a large wall painting and gold-toned mirror. A smooth black counter is at the eating bar. In addition, a sleek black bar with a small refrigerator tucked underneath adds a nice touch to the place.

A huge picture window, protected by thick drapes and a soft white second drape underneath allows each person in the room to enjoy taking a look at multi-colored city lights, along with buses, cars and taxi cabs on streets below.

Black rugs give a daring accent to the decorating theme, as they lay on shiny floors. Luxurious tubs with many jet sprays are in two bathrooms. Gorgeous fixtures are in the bathrooms too, along with marbleized counters.

Baby and I will be fine, here in this exquisite penthouse room at The Mirage.

Her Mommy and Daddy can have a good time in the city.
Let them be out for hours.

Baby and I will play and relax in this fine room. Yes, we will be just fine – what a treat!

MGM Grand – an 11th Floor Room

There is a deep window ledge to sit on as hotel guests peer
out of a large picture window, surrounded by luxuriously
heavy flower-print drapes.

This is quite a spacious room: pleasant and serene, with a
charming forest green sofa. The plush matching chair is
perfect for relaxing in after the rushing around that tourists
tend to do in Las Vegas, Nevada.

Reddish-brown mahogany furniture gives a decorators touch
in a sophisticated alcove, with pieces that include an end table,
a tea table with chairs, two large dressers and not one television
set, but two.

I gaze, fascinated, at upholstered raspberry colored chairs and
elegant lamps, scattered around the room. And then I notice
with delight subtle berry flowers splashed with pink accents
in the light-brown carpet over thick padding underneath.

Identical king sized beds, supported by sturdy headboards
lend a royal feeling to the cozy bedroom area. Wall hangings
are fun to look at. Chic eggshell wallpaper is on every wall
and there is ample space for clothes in a hallway closet.

White marbleized counters, along with two sparkling sinks give
a lavish aura to the large bathroom, which has a deep tub with
jet sprays, ready to turn on at any time.

A gleaming shower stall is separate from the tub, offering appealing choices for bathing enjoyment.

And there's more: black diamond-shaped designs in white tiled walls are unique. Matching diamonds are found in the soft-beige colored tile floor. Very nice!

Wonderful romantic views at night can't be beat: fairy-tale like spires proudly displaying glowing blues and oranges on top of the 'castle' known as the Excalibur Hotel makes one think of stories from Camelot so long ago.

Viewed from a different angle is the fabulous New York, New York Hotel and Casino, along with a multitude of cars, moving down brightly lit Tropicana Avenue.

Superb elegance – in a room on the 11th floor – a fine room, a grand room, at MGM Grand Hotel.

It's great to be on Las Vegas Boulevard, in the neon city known as "The Entertainment Capital of the World."

Life's a Trip, Pack Plenty of Bagels

Smooth hardwood floors, inviting study tables and solid wood chairs add nice touches to the bustling bagel shop. It has a fine location: across from the UNLV campus on Maryland Parkway.

Over 20 kinds of freshly-baked bagels are ready to be munched on, along with sandwiches and other tasty choices on the menu.

Groups of students linger in the shop, along with all sorts of people from the community in general.

How about tasting the coffee of the day: house, decaf, dark or sweet. There are some amazing bagel choices: Nutty Banana, Chocolate Chip, Sesame Dip'd, even delectable Wild Strawberry.

"What kind of cream cheese would you like?" asks a clerk, as she moves from one customer to the next in line. Mm – such mouth-watering delights. Should it be Chive, Raisin, Maple Walnut or Wild Berry Lite?

Piped music encompasses the small restaurant as people study, chat with one another, stay awhile. For those who prefer to be outside, a few tables and chairs are available.

In the early evening air, hilarious sprays of steam appear to be rolling out of the roof. What an interesting atmosphere!

Walls are painted a cheerful yellow daffodil color. At time musicians entertain customers for an hour or two. One guy plays a saxophone, another plays a guitar and the duo blend the music in pleasant harmony.

"Are you done with USA Today?" a student asks politely. "Go ahead," a woman replies, as she glances at the Wall Street Journal, the LA Times and a slightly wrinkled Las Vegas Review-Journal.

There used to be a fascinating sketch on a wall that I really enjoyed. It was a picture of a black and white cow jumping over a yellow moon with these words emblazoned above:

"Life's a trip, pack plenty of bagels."

Smiles and Tears

Sadness

Sadness is like a secret that wants to be released from hiding within one's inner being.

Sadness is a longing in the eyes, a painful ache in the heart, and no matter how one tries to smile, laugh, talk gaily or say nothing at all – it cannot be hidden.

Sometimes great music makes one sad, such as hearing a symphony piece or listening to romantic mood songs.

Sadness comes with a yearning to see a cherished friend, experience once again a gentle embrace – a burning desire to hear his voice, see his warm smile and touch the long fingers on his hand.

Sadness comes when one realizes that they are far away from God the Heavenly Father. His sense of closeness was so real that some would say, "Look at her, such joy she has! Where does it come from?"

Oh, I know – occasionally I hear, "Be thankful for the winter with it's dreary, cloudy days and the nasty weather: for later, spring in all of it's beauty is so lovely and meaningful."

But I say, "Why not have spring and summer all year long? Why have drab, gray winter at all?" Which is better? I don't know. Who does know?

A few people try to overcome sadness with funny jokes and splendid bits of acting as if real life is revolving on a stage, so they must perform – for no one can know how truly sad they are.

Others find a bit of comfort for the soul in worship services at church and singing songs of praise to God.

Then there are those who challenge sadness with work, more work. But after all, what happens to the person who is busy from early morning until very late at night, but the sense of despondency does not leave them?

This one thing is for certain: sadness does go away. It may take a fond embrace from a loved one, or just plain time.

So voila! – whether it be one hour, one day, or one enlightening moment: the sorrow is replaced by joy, peace, wonderment of all creation – and cleansing laughter.

Happiness

Happiness is the excitement of finding a new love,
or the joyous rejuvenation of an old one.

Happiness is seeing the twinkle in his eyes and knowing
that your eyes are twinkling brightly too.

Happiness is seeing your little girl's broad smile and hearing
her say, "I love you, Mommy."

Happiness is having a close friend bear with you through
the ups and downs of life – nearly all of them.

Happiness is waking up in the morning, stretching out your
muscles and declaring boldly, "I look forward to this day."

Happiness is being thankful for the hard, hurting experiences
in life: for after you have been through them, there is a sense
of compassion for others you did not have before.

Happiness is being free to be honest about your thoughts
and feelings, however strange they may seem.

Happiness is fleeting, elusive. It is not always with you – but
when it is, be glad and rejoice in it.

Goodbye, Daddy

Goodbye, Daddy. I hate to see you go. You had so many interesting stories to tell, so much in life to enjoy.

Goodbye, Daddy. I will miss you. Yes, all of us in the family will miss you.

Your favorite chair is empty now. No longer will I see you, glancing out of the big picture window, looking to see who is happily bounding up the familiar steps.

I wish that I would have loved you more, Daddy – to have kissed your cheek more, to have hugged you more, and given thanks for all you did for me and mine.

That is natural, I suppose. Most children wish for this, when death takes a parent away, far away.

I saw you trust God for miracles, awesome miracles in your life. You trusted Him, and he acted. He gave you victory over difficult habits and a ministry to the lost, the painfully hurting ones in this world.

You have been a man of faith, faith in the love of Christ our Lord. And you possessed an unshakeable belief in the sovereignty of a mighty God.

"I'm only a sinner saved by grace," you would softly say to me on some days. Daddy, you have been special to the Lord, for He loves sinners most of all.

He has had his arms stretched out to you. Now he is holding you close to him. He comforts you now Daddy, now that you are 'home' with him.

I will miss you now, but I will see you again. I will see you in heaven, where we will have eternity to share with Jesus, our everlasting, loving Lord.

Isn't that fantastic – wonderful – truly glorious? See you, Daddy. We will see you in eternity. Praise God!

In honor of Vern A. Loukojarvi
His funeral was on Sept. 21, 1981.

At the Court House

She parked her car several blocks away from the looming old Court House. She felt nervous, even apprehensive. Should she really go through with this?

Moist tears were stinging her eyes. She must ignore them and go on with life. Go on – but how? She had been a 'homemaker' and devoted to him for years.

She awkwardly approached the Recorder's Desk. Then she pensively showed her divorce papers to a busy office clerk.

"Where do I go for 'ex parte' matters?" she inquired.
"The clerk next door will help you," was the quick reply.

Didn't they know – didn't they care? How could those women behind the counters so casually press date stamps on papers and write down case numbers in a book, just as if it's the ordinary thing to do each and every working day of the week?

Lives were going to be irreparably changed forever. Marriages were so easily ended with the mere shuffling of papers, people going through a "Waiting Time" and then a judge signing the Final Decree. How sad.

There was a small flurry of activity as a group of divorce petitioners in a similar situation entered the strangely quiet room. They were different ages and nationalities, yet they were united at that hour: The Immediate Goal.

A man took the papers out of her hands, walked briskly
forward to the judge. The judge hardly glanced at her
as she anxiously waited for her turn. He quickly scribbled
his signature on the request. She was sent on her way.

Back downstairs, the woman found that the certified copies
of her petition were finally done. The divorce papers were
given an official case number: darkly stamped on the front.

"Are you going to have the sheriff serve him?"
She solemnly replied, "No, a process server."

Brief instructions were given to her, then she rushed to the
doors, to get outside – for she must smell some fresh air!

As she managed to get to her car in a mental haze and
misty eyelids, she thought to herself : Yes, I had to do it.
Yes, I will be alright. It is okay to start a new life, to aim
for a new sense of direction.

When she drove to her own place – the home occupied now
by only herself – she was filled with sorrow and yet, somehow
relieved. It was done.

Baby Birds
and
Alluring Animals

"Hooter" and "Tooter"

Two small baby owls –fluffy, appealing and several weeks
old; with four sharp talons on each foot, sturdy enough to
grab onto our waiting fingers.

Fascinating colored feathers: brown, black, beige, and a
sparkling white. Round eyes of golden yellow; dark pupils
that grow larger or smaller, depending on reflected light.

Home at last, with the unique little birds: who stare at us
with great curiousity. They are never mean at all, never
use their strong beaks to strike at us or hurt our skin.

"Wouldn't bugs taste good to them?" the children ask. We
want to experiment, offering assorted foods at the end of
our fingertips: steak, peas, even some wriggly earth worms.

The family gazes in amusement as the tiny ground owls
turn their heads all the way around – with no effort at all,
it seems.

"Do you have a medicine dropper?" is asked at the pharmacy.
It is small – just right for giving the owls some water. They
crane their heads upward, grateful for refreshing, cool water.

It is not long until the two of them are impatient with the
ugly cardboard box, the confining prison. "Hooter" and
"Tooter" make active, loud noises at night; nocturnal birds
at their best.

Occasionally in the daytime we let them fly around in the apartment with a swift whiff whiff sound.

We look for the cute little fellows. They land in all sorts of places; on top of the refrigerator, on top of bathroom bars, and on a bookcase in the living room.

Wow! At times we let them perch on our shoulders, our hands or someone's head. They are tremendously funny and curious as they can be.

Fear of people is nothing to them. Fear of dogs or cats is quite another matter.

One day "Hooter" was out on the front lawn when a skittish poodle barked near his little head.

The challenge was on! Vigorously fluffing his feathers out and fanning his wings – boldly spreading them as far as they could go, he angrily shrieked at the circling dog.

The dog backed off, then advanced forward. At last the precious owl was rescued, picked up and held closely.

Fly – fly – they long to fly, to soar through the air and to be free. We are sorry. The time has come for our wild pets to have a home of their own.

We climb into the family jeep, then drive out to sagebrush and vast, open fields. A mama owl is close by, circling high above us, appearing to be quite nervous.

We take some last-minute pictures with our camera, and then – into the hole in the ground they go. Freedom is theirs at last. The two of them pause, look back at us. What is going on? They seem to ask us.

We slowly drive away, knowing that all we have left of our adorable little birds are wonderful, fun-filled memories.

A Prize Pet Indeed

'Bingo' the black and white farm dog rushed forward,
nearly bursting with excitement – loudly barking as he
went, while sniffing the path in front of him.

Rose hurried to catch up with him, teeming with childhood
energy. Why was her dog barking so much? she wondered.

Around protective oak trees with crunchy puffballs underneath
her shoes – through scratchy bushes and tall grass – the two
of them ran some more, when – suddenly they stopped.

When the girl saw what her border collie had found, her heart
leaped with joy. Oh, my! She had wanted a pet like that for
a long time.

He was so beautiful, so sleek and shiny, with blended hues of
black and white. She would catch him, take him home. What
a prize pet he would be. A prize pet indeed!

The narrow-nosed animal dug fiercely into the bushes and
soft ground. Her dog darted forward, then he jumped back.
The frightened critter dug his feet deeper into the thin grass.
If only she could get near that tail of his, and simply grab
onto him –

"E-e-k!" the girl screamed, as 'Bingo' scrambled away from
her. A strange-smelling spray was all over her. It stung her
eyes, it was clinging to her clothes. The awful odor was
almost too much to bear.

Despairingly, she turned on her heels to run home as fast as her legs would go. The dog was bounding along right behind her.

Mother was working on the lawn. As Rose ran to her mother for comfort, she was met with disbelief and instant rejection.

"Oh, no. You've been near a nasty skunk. You can't go into the house, not smelling like that."

If only she could get rid of the stench, the horrible smell! Full of tears, the girl disrobed in the old woodshed.

Mother prepared steamy bath water, pouring it into a large wood tub. Mother acted as if she was not pleased at all.

Poor 'Bingo' was not petted for days. At last, to the farm girl's relief – no smell was noticeable on her dog.

She was glad about that, but disappointed that her shiny black skunk, the little darling – with the white stripe down his back would never be her pet – never.

With a sense of chagrin, she often recalled that day, the day that her prize pet got away.

"Little One"

A scream could be heard, wafting on the wind.
  "No, Jake – no. Put it down, Jake."

The loud scream seemed to be too late. The baby
goose was in the jaws of the dog. It's thin neck was
drooping sideways, while the dog ran ahead of the
anxious man.

At last – my husband touched the dog and found that
the little gosling was still alive. Jake's jaws were gentle,
drawing no blood.

"Let go, Jake, let go," he firmly commanded the family
dog.

He tenderly folded the small bird in his arms, brought it
up to the pickup truck and placed the bird onto my lap.
The goose was wet and very frightened, but definitely
still alive.

"We can take him home to care for him; we just can't
leave him here, not like this."

During the drive to our house, the little bird got dry.
We could see gray-yellow down all over his delicate body.
Tiny wings were taking shape. He was just a baby, that
was for sure.

We made a bed for the small gosling in a box, kept him
warm as we could, but not too warm. The four children
gathered around him, gazing curiously into the box.

"Will he eat some lettuce – maybe some hamburger?"
With gentle coaxing, they were able to feed him a few
tasty tidbits.

After a couple of days, we took him out to see the chickens
and place him in the noisy chicken yard. The gosling did
not like that idea at all. No way! They were not his kind.

Full of cockiness, the husky red rooster stared at this
strange bird. Whoops, mistake. The little goose snapped
at him with his beak. We laughed as Jake ran back and
forth, near the strong wire fence.

"What shall we name him?" the children asked me one
balmy day. "Little One," I replied. "That's a silly name,"
one of them commented. Silly or not, that is what our
pet was affectionately called from then on.

As the days led into weeks, we noticed some changes
that occurred right before our eyes.

"His wings are a lot bigger and his feet are big now."
"And he's getting real feathers," I heard.

The dog was either tied up, or warned, "Be gentle."
Thin weeds were delectable to the growing Canada
goose. So were leaves on bushes – and those darn
dandelions.

With a sense of light fear, one night we left him alone
in the back yard.

As we peeked out of the kitchen window, "Little One" got closer to Jake, who slowly chased him around the yard. Then the dog casually laid down to go to sleep.

The confidant goose rested right beside him. What a surprise! The dog and the bird became the best of friends after that. Our special pet definitely preferred the dog's company to those stupid, gawky chickens!

The time came for us to move far away. A decision had to be made – and soon.

"What shall we do with the goose?"

A Utah farmer nearby was known to have all sorts of animals on his land. We decided to visit him one day. We noticed a nice mixture of domestic geese and wild ones, waddling around in a field near his house.

He told us this story: a wild Canada goose acted like he wanted to stay on his farm for quite awhile. One bleak day the big bird scanned the skies, observing a gaggle of geese, flying high in the sky above him.

They were raucously honking to one another as they flew in a V-shape pattern. Suddenly he was up in the sky, making a lot of commotion as if to say, "Wait for me."

The farmer was sorry to see him go. Six months went by. A year went by. His favorite goose was gone forever.

One morning he did a double-take as he looked over the collection of birds in his pasture. The goose who flew away so long ago was back!

This time the handsome gander decided that this was the place for him. He never did take off with wild geese again.

"Would you take our pet goose?" we asked the farmer. "Sure, no problem," was the prompt reply.

My husband lifted "Little One" up and over the rustic wood fence. With a swift motion, he threw the goose down to the abundant grass below.

"Little One" surveyed his surroundings. There were so many birds. He was astonished. They were his kind! They looked just like him!

Quick as a wink, he ran over to the group and joined right in. We left the farm, knowing that he was happy at last.

Wind Whistling Through Her Hair

A narrow dirt trail, covered with grass. Leaving the barn area, going down small hills. Crossing a narrow white bridge with silent frogs hiding in still waters.

"Jody" the rich deep brown horse with black mane so finely roached, strains forward, walking up the hill, then on to a gold straw-filled crackly sounding field.

Blue sky, small white clouds gently moving in soft puffy shapes. Fresh, clear early evening air; all part of the rider's world.

"Jody" gradually changes from walking to a vigorous trot as the rider bounces lightly on the saddle. A lowering of the reins, a click of the tongue – a sign is given that the gentle mare easily recognizes.

The rider rises up above the saddle as her horse increases speed, galloping forward, smoothly and effortlessly. The mare's back legs nearly meet her front legs as she lunges onward, gliding across expansive pasture land.

The woman happily revels in the experience of feeling the wind whistling through her hair as she travels along with the galloping, galloping horse.

A turn around is made and the two horses reverse their path, back to the original dirt trail.

Down and up gently sloping hills, past the weather-beaten
barn, they go. Then to the large white farm house, a very
welcome sight indeed.

Her escort takes the firm metal bit out of his horse's mouth
and commands "Saint" to stand still. Then he loosens the
rust-hued straps, pulls the saddle and blanket off.

He ties the dapple-gray horse to a thick, gnarled tree.
Plenty of rope is left, so that the stallion can relish eating
lush lawn grass and a few ripening pears.

"Can you get down?" he inquires. She flips her right leg over,
confidently meeting the left. In a moment, she is down to
the ground, with the help of leaning on her friend's shoulder.

The brown mare is taken care of. All paraphernalia is removed.
Her rider gently leads her under trees and up to the gate. She
is taken through and released out into an inviting pasture.

The horse is free at last: to run and to frolic as she likes.

Glimpses of Life

Going to College

Going to college, the center of learning, when one is "old" – a 36 year old mother with three children and bills to pay, no less.

Free to exercise and let the mind be turning, always turning. Excited, anxious too, when answering lots of test questions.

Sociology; what is that anyway? Stations in life, norms and role conflict. Stratification and coercion. There are so many terms to investigate and try to understand.

Journalism class, learning about reporting, with a chance to write articles for the college newspaper. What a challenge!

"A lead should capture your reader's attention."
"Get the Who – What – Why – and the Where."

Beginning Tennis; beginner, that's true. Getting in shape, as the days of the week go by. "Run twice around the gym," we are told by the instructor. We rush outside to the dark green tennis courts.

After practice, it's time to compete against other teams. We have a chance to accrue some decent points in the game. Love, Fifteen, Thirty, Forty, Deuce: and we're tied. Ad in – now just one more point. Game. Aha, we won!

Office Management; learning about noise control and
lighting, along with machines and methods. Looking at
Theory X and Theory Y of human behavior. This is
quite relevant, really.

Taking time to study, to ponder life on the campus in
the quiet library, amidst tables, chairs and many books.

Trying to achieve balance between homework, kids,
housework and meeting with friends. Must not forget
the Work-Study program: typing for teachers in the
afternoons.

Mother, from others you may get some looks: friendly,
wondering, admiring, curious, accepting.

What was that phrase that you heard recently?
  Oh, yes. Just a 'late bloomer' you are.

A Secretary's Day

Set the typewriter margins and line up the paper.
She types the best way she can, hoping for no mistakes.
Then the noisy telephone rings again. The sound forces
her to leave the trail of thoughts that she had.

   "Foster and Blake, how may I help you?"
   That phrase is so monotonous, so familiar.

Time to be quickly organized: put those forms, and
documents, along with purchase orders in correct order.
Some of them are numerical and others are alphabetical
in nature. Trips to the copy machine seem to be an all
day event.

Now for a coffee break – a chance to catch up on "the
latest" from the other girls in the office. After draining
her cup, she feels alert and ready to get back to work.

With a sense of anxiety, she glances at the dictating
machine, which has a cassette tape in it. Other tapes
are nearby. How will she finish typing all of them
before the end of the day?

While pressing a foot pedal underneath her desk, she
listens to the boss's words: some are clear and crisp,
while others seem to be a bit garbled, not making
much sense.

"Correction – would my secretary please omit that last
paragraph? Darn it! He would change his mind.

Why can't there be some pizzazz in the office furniture around here? - she wonders as she looks at the ugly green filing cabinets and a collection of boring potted plants.

"Let me see soft pink walls and frilly lace curtains!" she longs to cry out. This place is so drab, not like her warm, cozy home that she likes so much.

Envelopes are addressed and 'the boss' has signed all of his daily correspondence. The mail is finally in order. She walks to the mail room, pausing to greet a coworker with a smile.

Catching up on last-minute details, she places file folders into her wire basket, ready for tomorrow's tasks. With a flourish, she places the gray plastic cover over the typewriter that has been turned off.

Quitting time, according to the round black clock that is on the white wall. Oh, good!

Sighing with relief, the secretary finally goes outside, and gets into her car. At home she relaxes in a refreshingly different world.

Lady in Distress

She gets into her car, runs the engine, warming it up for action on the road. She pulls out onto the street and looks forward to a long, waiting highway. The steady hum of the motor sounds good.

Oh, oh – a wiggly jiggle – an awful sounding bump is heard. The ride is no longer smooth at all. In fact, it is quite frightening, even a bit weird.

"I've got a flat tire!" she yells out loud to herself.

It's time to pull over to the shoulder of the highway and stop the car, get out, pull up the hood to signal for help, if there is any.

She gets back into her car, wondering, "What is the best thing to do?"

Numerous drivers whiz past her. No one stops. Whoosh, Whoosh – she hears: over and over again. What now?

She glances in her rearview mirror, spotting a pickup truck that is slowing down, even coming to a real stop. A short mother, a small child and a young father are in the truck.

The man asks the distressed lady, "What is wrong?" Then he glances at a terribly flat tire, with shredded pieces lying along the roadside gravel.

"I have a jack in my trunk," she says to him.
The two of them peer into the open trunk.

"Think I will use my own jack," he replies.

His deft fingers move in concentrated action. He
removes the tire out of the large trunk. Then he
proceeds to get the spare tire on the wheel, and he
jiggles it vigorously until – it fits!

"Thank you so much!" she exclaims, grateful that he
had stopped. He accepts no payment, no offering.
He simply smiles warmly and says, "Have a nice day."

The man gets into his truck with his patiently waiting
family. They quickly drive away, complete strangers
to her. She marvels at his kindness, then starts up her
engine and drives smoothly down the inviting highway.

Mama's Red Wool Dress

Mama's red wool dress was lying there, on top of
Mama's bed, in her fragrant-smelling bedroom. Her
17-year old daughter caressed it with her fingers as
she imagined the pretty garment on her shapely
young body.

The slim lines – the stylish look – if only it could be
hers for one single day. "Mother, may I borrow your
dress sometime?" she wanted to ask. Of course,
the answer would be no.

One delightful Saturday, Mama truly surprised her.
 "Yes, Rose, you can borrow my red wool dress."

The teenager was so excited! She quickly tried it on and
gazed at herself in a long mirror. She liked what she saw:
flattering, that was the word.

Next she walked down a busy street. The girl wistfully
looked into a few store windows. She sauntered along
sidewalks, trying to avoid wildly flirting fellows, who
were cruising slowly past her in their cars.

On Sunday there was church to attend, where she
could mingle with friends and sing in the Youth Group.
She wore the dress again, admiring the fluffy white
angora, which surrounded the neckline.

When she sat down on a metal chair, Dick quietly began
to whisper to her.

"I saw you yesterday, walking down Liberty Street.
You were wearing that red dress and I nearly drove my
car into a telephone pole."

His cheeks turned a bright pink as he looked down on
the floor. The girl turned to hide her amusement as
she turned around to face him. Then she lowered her
eyes, with a shy smile on her lips.

In later years she would recall the day that Mama let
her borrow the soft red wool dress and how she made
heads turn as she walked – simply walked down the
street.

Bird on a Fence Post, Poetry
How to order additional books:
http://www.dancingrosebooks.com
ISBN: 978-0-9796147-0-5
Write to: Rose Anne Dane,
PO Box 5973, Salem OR 97304